I Can Tap into GREATNESS

Power
Strength Joy
Courage Peace
Self-Control
Love Faith

Jackie Clyburn

ISBN 979-8-89243-816-2 (paperback)
ISBN 979-8-88943-857-1 (hardcover)
ISBN 979-8-88943-856-4 (digital)

Christian Faith Publishing
832 Park Avenue
Meadville, PA 16335
www.christianfaithpublishing.com

Printed in the United States of America

Dedication

I dedicate this book to my grandchildren Noa
and Shiloh. "Always know that you are immensely
blessed, highly favored and deeply loved."

Inspiration

To my husband, Terry, my son Terrence, my daughter
Christina and to all the children of Exceptionalities, that
I have taught over the past 20 years, you have inspired
me to never give up, push through any challenges
and to trust God because He made you and I,
GREAT!

I can tap into greatness
because greatness is in me!

Power
Peace
Joy
Love
Faith
Strength
Courage

When I feel overwhelmed...
You Can't
You will Never
I am Greater
I can't
"Oh, No! This is too hard."
..."I'm so nervous."

Memory verse: "I can do all things through Christ because he gives me strength" (Philippians 4:13 ICB).

When I feel afraid...

WE GOT YOU NOW...
YOU ARE TRAPPED!!
HELP!!
Scared

I can tap into greatness.
I am strong and brave.
(Joshua 1:9 ICB).
Jesus is
with me
Faith
Courage
Memory verse: "God did not give me a spirit that makes me afraid. He gave me a spirit of power and love and self-control" (2 Timothy 1:7 ICB).

When I feel sad...
Nobody cares

I can tap into greatness.

The Lord protects and defends me. (Psalm 28:7 ICB).

Memory verse: Give all your worries to Him because He cares for you (1 Peter 5:7 ICB).

When I feel angry...

I can tap into greatness.

Love does not remember wrongs done against it (1 Corinthians 13:5 ICB).

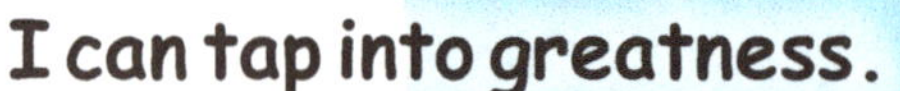

Memory verse: "In this world you will have trouble. But be brave! I have defeated the world" (John 16:33 ICB).

When I feel lonely...
No Friends

I can tap into greatness.
God has chosen me (John 15:16 ICB).
God chose me... I am His!
Accepted
Loved
Memory verse: If God be for me, then no one can defeat me (Romans 8:31 ICB).

Memory verse: "God's Spirit, who is in me, is greater than the devil, who is in the world" (1 John 4:4 ICB).

Remember Who You Are!

I am great!
I am great because greatness is in me.
I am great because I have a great mind. I can solve
problems and learn. I make the right choices.
I am great because I have a great heart. I love
myself and others. I respect people.
I am great because I have a great body. I am strong!
I have the power to push through the pain.
I am disciplined.
I am great!

About the Author

Jackie Clyburn is a mother of two, a grandmother, and a teacher. She has taught children with exceptionalities for over twenty years and has come to realize that we are more alike than different. With each new day comes its own set of fears, anxiety, and unknown challenges that we must face no matter how inadequate we may feel for the tasks ahead. But she has learned that God has given her all that she needs to overcome every challenge and be a victor—"more than a conqueror." In her life, she has only been able to accomplish any success (fulfilling His purpose) with His helper, the Holy Spirit. It's when she surrenders her will, emotions, and all that she is to Him, so that she is able to receive all that He is in her. Only then can she realize His greatness in areas she could only imagine. It is with Holy Spirit that she is able to complete this work. She gives God all the glory, all the honor, and all the praise for what He has done in her life. She prays that this book will teach, encourage, and remind all His children, young and old, to tap into the greatness of God within them.

Receive and be blessed!